Kirklees
METROPOLITAN COUNCIL
CULTURAL SERVICES

Cultural Services Headquarters,
Red Doles Lane,
Huddersfield. West Yorks. HD2 1YF

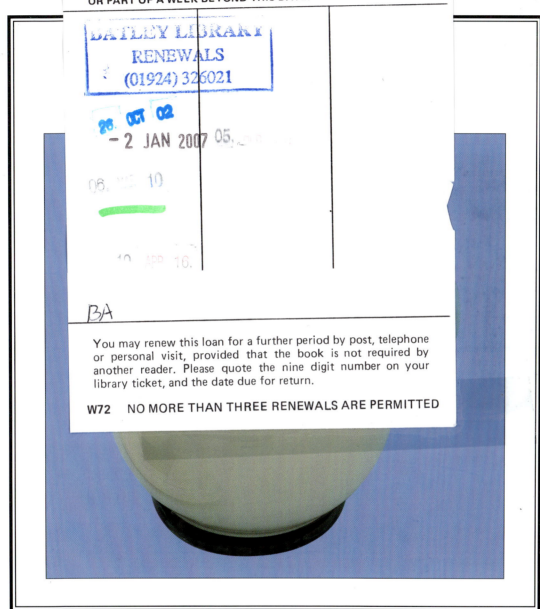

Jillian Powell

HODDER
Wayland

an imprint of Hodder Children's Books

Titles in the series

BREAD   EGGS   FISH   FRUIT
MILK   PASTA   POTATOES
POULTRY   RICE   VEGETABLES

First published in Great Britain in 1996 by Wayland (Publishers) Ltd
Reprinted in 2001 by Hodder Wayland, an imprint of Hodder Children's Books

© Hodder Wayland 1996

Hodder Children's Books,
A division of Hodder Headline Ltd
338 Euston Road
London NW1 3BH

Series Editor: Sarah Doughty
Editor: Liz Harman
Design: Jean Wheeler
Illustration: Peter Bull
Cover: Zul Mukhida – assistant photostylist Bridget Tily

British Library Cataloguing in Publication Data
Powell, Jillian
Milk. – (Food)
1. Milk – Juvenile literature
2. Cookery (Milk) – Juvenile literature
I. Title
641.3'521

ISBN 0 7502 3451 2

Typeset by Jean Wheeler

Printed and bound in Italy by L.E.G.O. S.p.A., Vicenza

Picture acknowledgements

Cephas 4 (bottom), 9 (bottom), 18 (bottom), 21 (bottom), 24; Chapel Studios
12 (top), 15 (top), 16–17, 17 (right), 18 (top), 20 (bottom), 22 (top), 23 (top);
James Davis Travel Photography 9 (top), 23 (bottom); E T Archive 6 (bottom);
Mary Evans 7 (top), 14 (bottom); Eye Ubiquitous 4 (top), 8 (top), 22 (bottom),
25 (both); Michael Holford 6 (top); Life File 10 (left), 12 (bottom), 16 (left);
National Dairy Council 5, 7 (bottom), 11, 13 (top), 14 (top), 15 (bottom), 19 (top),
21 (top); Wayland Picture Library title page, contents page, 8 (bottom), 10 (right),
13 (bottom), 19 (bottom), 20 (top).

Contents

Our first food

Milk is the first food we are given as babies. All mammals, including humans, begin life drinking their mother's milk. The milk that a mother makes in her body protects her baby from germs and is very nutritious.

▲ Like this pig, all female mammals produce milk to feed their young.

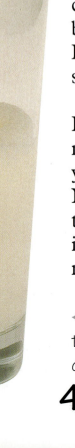

Most of the milk we drink comes from cows but people around the world drink many types of milk. In India, the Far East and the Pacific countries, people milk the water buffaloes that work in the rice fields. In many mountain areas, goats and sheep provide milk.

In the Himalaya and Andes mountains, people drink milk from yaks and llamas. In Saudi Arabia and North Africa, the Bedouin and other tribal peoples drink camels' milk and in Mongolia and parts of Russia, nomadic peoples drink horses' milk.

◀ Milk is a meal in a glass. It is one of the best foods because it contains lots of nutrients and is easy to digest.

We can drink milk hot or cold and use it in drinks such as milk shakes, tea and coffee or in soups and sauces, waffles, pancakes, custard, ice-cream and rice puddings. Milk is also made into dairy foods like cream, butter, cheese, and yoghurt.

▲ A selection of dairy products. Foods made from milk include yoghurt, butter, cream and cheese.

Milk in the past

This ancient Egyptian wall painting shows farmers counting their cattle. Cattle were kept for their milk and meat and were very valuable.

The Egyptian queen, Cleopatra, who lived in the first century BC is said to have bathed in asses' milk to whiten her skin.

People have been milking animals for thousands of years. About 4,000 years ago, nomadic peoples in Asia and the Middle East carried dried or fermented milk in bottles made from clay, animal skins or gourds. The ancient Greeks and Romans drank milk from goats, sheep and asses.

In the Middle Ages, milk and dairy foods were called 'white meats'. Peasant families kept a cow on village grazing land and made cream, butter, cheese and buttermilk. Milk was used in sweet and savoury puddings, in thick soups called pottages and in posset, a kind of drink fermented with ale. Junkets, made from milk curds mixed with sugar and rosewater, were popular for festivals and fairs.

A milkmaid in 1805. Milkmaids carried milk in pails hung over their shoulders and sold cups of milk in the street.

6

▲ A Victorian milkman.

Cows' milk gradually became more popular than sheep's or goats' milk. Cows grazed on grassland near towns and the milk was sold at farms or markets.

By the seventeenth century, some farms sent milk up to the towns, carried by a rider on a horse. Milk was sold from churns in the street and from dairy shops. Cowkeepers kept cows in stalls behind the shops. People brought their own jugs to be filled. Often the milk was mixed with water and was full of germs.

After about 1800, there were bigger dairy farms. The farmers sold milk to milk traders. The traders employed milkmaids to sell milk in the street and door-to-door.

By the middle of the nineteenth century, the railways were used to transport fresh milks. Milk sellers used handcarts and later horse-drawn milk floats to deliver milk to people's homes.

In the twentieth century, vans and lorries, and later electric milk floats began to be used. Milk was sold in sealed glass bottles which could be washed and re-used.

▼ An early twentieth-century horse-drawn milk cart. The milk was kept in the big churn in the cart.

7

What is milk?

All female mammals, including goats, sheep, cats, dogs, mice and whales, produce milk. People drink milk from cows, goats, sheep, buffaloes, horses, camels, llamas, yaks and reindeer. Milk varies with the type of animal and the food it is fed.

▲ Around the world, people drink milk from many animals. This woman in Tibet is milking a yak.

Dairy farmers keep cows for milking. A cow must have mated with a bull and given birth to a calf before she can make milk. For the first few days, the calf drinks its mother's milk, then the farmer feeds the calf and sells the cow's milk. The mother cow will go on making milk for about ten months after her calf is born.

◀ A cow with her calf. Calves are born in the spring or autumn.

A cow can eat about 70 kg of grass each day.

Cows make milk from grass and water. The cow tears off grass with her tongue and swallows it into two of her four stomachs, called the rumen and the reticulum.

From time to time, the partly digested grass returns to the cow's mouth for her to chew. This is called chewing the cud. The cow then swallows the grass again and it passes into her third stomach, the omasum, then the fourth, the abomasum, where it is digested. Milk is stored in the cow's udder.

In winter, cows are fed on hay (dried grass) or silage (pickled grass), and given nutritious animal feed like cereal cake.

▶ In South-east Asia and India coconut milk is often used for cooking. This woman from Thailand is removing the hard shells of fresh coconuts.

Soya 'milk' is made from crushed soya beans and is widely used around the world, especially in Asia. In Europe and America, nut milk has been made for many years by crushing and soaking nuts. Amerindians used pecan and hickory nuts.

The food in milk

Milk is a natural and nutritious food. It contains protein, fat and carbohydrate as well as vitamins and minerals.

Milk is an important source of calcium, which makes strong bones and teeth. A pint of milk gives us the calcium we need each day, although children and women who are breastfeeding babies may need more. Milk contains a protein, called casein, which helps to make our bones and muscles strong and gives us energy.

▲ Milk is especially important for babies and children because it helps to build a healthy body with strong muscles, bones and teeth.

◄ Milk is easy to digest so it is a useful food for people who are ill or elderly.

Milk contains vitamins and minerals which we need to keep us healthy. Vitamin A helps healthy growth, skin and eyes. Vitamin B_1 keeps the nervous system healthy and helps the body to take energy from carbohydrate foods. Vitamin B_2 helps us to take energy from fats and proteins, and vitamin B_{12} helps us to grow and keeps red blood cells and the nervous system working properly. Vitamin D helps make healthy bones.

▼ Dairy foods like milk, butter, cream, cheese and yoghurt can all form part of a healthy diet.

Milk contains about 3.9 per cent fat, which gives us energy, but too much fat can lead to heart disease. Some milk is sold with the fat content reduced. Semi-skimmed milk contains about 1.6 per cent fat. Skimmed milk has only 0.1 per cent fat. Semi-skimmed and skimmed milk contain the same amount of protein and calcium as whole milk and most vitamins except A and D. These are lost during the skimming process but sometimes extra milk solids and vitamins are added to skimmed milk to make it more nutritious.

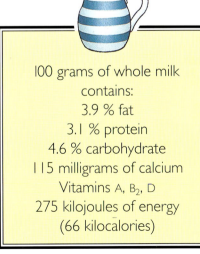

100 grams of whole milk
contains:
3.9 % fat
3.1 % protein
4.6 % carbohydrate
115 milligrams of calcium
Vitamins A, B_2, D
275 kilojoules of energy
(66 kilocalories)

How milk is produced

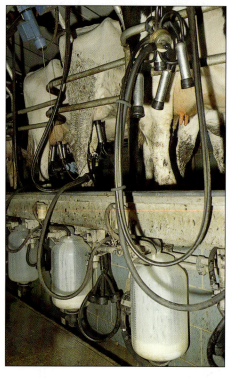

The cows in a dairy herd are milked twice a day, usually in the early morning and late afternoon. They come into the milking parlour in a set order. Each cow has an electronic tag in her ear so the farmer can check how much milk she is producing.

A cow makes about 10 to 15 litres of milk each day. She may be given extra feed to keep her healthy while she is being milked.

Cows are usually milked by machines which have cups that fit over the teats of the udder and suck out milk, just as a calf would do.

▲ Cows being milked using a milking machine. The milk is piped into a large glass jar which records the amount each cow produces.

▶ A Russian woman milking a cow by hand. On many farms around the world, cows are still milked in this way.

The farmer tests the milk to make sure it is safe to drink. The milk is piped into the farm vat where it is refrigerated at a temperature of 4.5° C or less.

The milking parlour is washed down and all the equipment sterilized every day so that no germs can get into the milk.

▲ This tanker driver is taking a sample of milk from a farm's vat.

Every day, a tanker comes to collect the milk. The driver pushes a switch to stir the milk in the vat and tests the temperature. The milk is sucked through a hose into the tanker. Once a week, a sample of milk is taken to a laboratory to be tested.

The tanker keeps the milk cold and can carry up to 9,000 litres of milk. At the dairy, the milk is piped into huge storage tanks called silos. The tanker is cleaned and sterilized ready to be used again.

▶ A tanker driver prepares to pipe milk from a farm's vat into a tanker. A flow meter measures the amount of milk collected from each farm.

Heat-treating milk

At the dairy, milk is heat treated to kill any harmful bacteria and help it to stay fresh. If not treated, the natural bacteria in milk will turn it sour, especially in warmth and light.

Most milk is heat treated in a process called pasteurization. A machine heats the milk to over 71° C for at least 15 seconds, then quickly cools it to below 10° C.

▼ This machine is called a heat exchanger. It is used to pasteurize milk by heating it then quickly cooling it.

The process of pasteurization is named after Louis Pasteur (1822–95), the French scientist who discovered the method in the 1860s.

Some milk is homogenized, which makes it easier to digest. The milk is passed through high pressure jets which break up the fat globules and mix the cream through the milk.

◄ Louis Pasteur.

14

◀ UHT milk is useful for cooking because it can be stored and will keep fresh until it is opened.

Milk given ultra heat treatment (UHT) can be stored in unopened containers for several months. This is useful in hot countries where people do not have refrigerators. The milk is heated to 132.2° C for a second or more, cooled, then packed in airtight boxes.

Some milk is sterilized. First it is homogenized, then bottled and steam heated to very high temperatures of up to 130° C, which kill all bacteria. Some vitamins are lost. Sterilized milk has a slightly sweet taste because the high temperature cooks the milk sugar. Sterilized milk can be stored unopened for two to three months.

Milk is packed in plastic or glass bottles, plastic lined cartons or cans. Modern machines fill up to 600 milk bottles a minute. Glass bottles can be washed and sterilized and recycled. Bottles are sealed with foil caps which are coloured to show the type of milk.

▼ Milk being poured into clean bottles at a dairy The machine also puts a foil cap on each bottle.

Processing milk

Some milk is canned as drinks, which may be flavoured with fruit or chocolate. Canned milk stays fresh for several months and is popular in hot countries.

Evaporated milk has been heated to remove water and thicken it. It is twice as concentrated as ordinary milk. The milk is evaporated at temperatures of 60–65° C, then homogenized and cooled. Machines pour the milk into cans which are sealed then sterilized at 115–120° C for ten minutes. The cans are cooled and labelled.

▲ This machine, at a dairy in Finland, is used to make dried milk products.

▶ Sweets like toffee, fudge, chocolate and coconut ice are made with milk or cream.

16

Condensed milk is evaporated milk which has been sweetened with sugar. It is three times as concentrated as ordinary milk. Milk is heat treated at 110–115° C for one or two minutes then homogenized. Sugar is added then the sweetened milk is evaporated at 55–60° C. It is quickly cooled, poured into cans and sealed. Condensed milk can be used for making sweets and in sweet dishes. It is widely used in parts of Asia, especially when fresh milk is not widely available.

▼ Dried milk powder is a useful replacement for fresh milk in hot drinks like tea and coffee.

Milk can be dried into a powder which is easy to store and can be mixed with water and used as milk. Milk is heat treated and homogenized, then dried by being sprayed into a heated tank or poured over heated rollers. The dried powder is packed into airtight containers. It contains all the goodness of fresh milk, except some vitamins, which may be added to make the powder more nutritious.

Dairy foods

Milk can be used to make dairy products like yoghurt, butter, cream and ice-cream.

Yogurt was first made by nomadic tribes in West Asia and Eastern Europe thousands of years ago. They used the stomachs of dead animals as bags to carry milk. As the milk was shaken up, a chemical called rennet in the stomach bag fermented the milk to make yoghurt.

Milk is used to make a wide range of dairy foods. Cream is made by heating milk to 50° C then piping it into giant machines which spin very fast to separate out the cream. The cream is then cooled to below 5° C and stored in cold tanks ready for pasteurization, sterilization or ultra heat treatment. Cream can be packed in tubs, cartons, tins and aerosol cans.

To make butter, cream is churned at high speed in spinning machines until the fat globules stick together. The butter is cooled, and may be salted before being cut and wrapped by machines. Over 11 litres of milk are needed to make one 500 g packet of butter

Butter, cream, yoghurt and ice-cream are still made by hand all over the world. This man is making butter at a small dairy in France.

As cream is churned, a watery liquid called whey is drained off. This may have a culture of harmless bacteria added to help it to ferment as buttermilk.

To make yoghurt, milk is thickened by evaporation, homogenized and heated to above, 85° C for 15 to 20 minutes, then quickly cooled. A culture is added which helps it ferment and set. Fruit and other flavours may also be added.

Ice-cream may have been made in China up to 5,000 years ago. The Italians began making ice-cream in the thirteenth century, and it was introduced to Britain 500 years later.

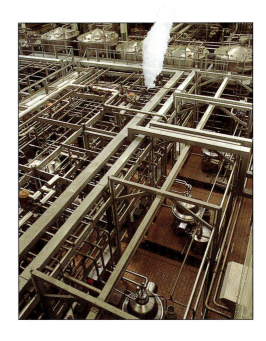

▲ Yoghurt-making equipment at a large factory.

▶ Ice-cream can be eaten as a snack or as a dessert. Ice-cream can be made in many flavours.

Making cheese

In big factories, milk for making cheese is pasteurized and pumped into vats. A culture is added to give the milk flavour and turn it slightly acid. Animal or vegetable rennet is then mixed in. The enzymes in the rennet separate the milk into thick curds and runny whey.

Curds and whey are stirred and heated, then the curds are blown to the top of a tall tower where they stick together as the whey drains off. Blocks of curd are cut into small pieces and sprayed with salt. Some cheeses have fruit, nuts or herbs added. The cheese is pressed into metal containers and wrapped.

Hard cheeses are stored at 5–10° C. The longer cheese is stored, the stronger its flavour. The cheese is then sliced and wrapped ready to be sold.

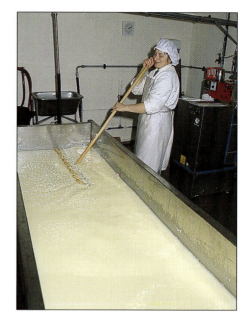

▲ This woman is stirring rennet into milk to separate it into curds and whey.

◀ A selection of some of the hundreds of different types of cheese from around the world.

◀ Making cheddar in the traditional way at a farmhouse cheese dairy.

▼ Goats'-milk cheese being made by hand in France.

Some dairies still make cheese the traditional way. The cheesemakers cut and stir the curds by hand, turning and stacking blocks of curd for up to an hour. This is called cheddaring. The blocks are cut into small pieces, mixed with salt and pressed into moulds lined with cloth for storage.

Pasteurized skimmed milk is used to make soft cheeses like cottage cheese. A culture and rennet are added to the milk to separate it, then the whey is drained off and the curds washed with cold water to give a crumbly fresh cheese. Some cheeses are made using sheep's or goats' milk, which gives them a different flavour.

Milk around the world

In Britain, Spain, France and Portugal milk is used to make creamy rice puddings, sweet custard flans and other sweet dishes. The French use cream to make sweet and savoury dishes richer. In Greece, a thick yoghurt made from sheep's or cows' milk is used in soups, salads and cooked dishes.

Americans use milk to make waffles and pancakes, which are traditionally served with maple syrup. In France, pancakes called crêpes are very popular. Pancakes are traditionally eaten on Shrove Tuesday in Britain.

▲ Crème caramel, a French dessert.

In the Middle East, yoghurt has been eaten since ancient times. It is made with milk from cows, sheep or buffaloes and is used in meat dishes, desserts, salad dressings and iced drinks.

◀ Pancakes and crêpes are popular in many countries. They can be sweet or savoury.

Yoghurt is used in soups in Russia. In Armenia, it is cooked with herbs and barley to make a dish called spass.

In Asia, milk and yoghurt are used for vegetarian dishes, desserts and fermented milk drinks. Many Indians start the day with a glass of frothy hot milk flavoured with nuts and saffron. Condensed milk, called khir, is used in cooking and buttermilk may be spiced and poured over plain rice.

Milk is used to make Asian curd cheeses like paneer and chhena. Chhena can be shaped into balls, hearts and diamonds, coloured with vegetable dyes, and boiled in syrup to make sweets. The sweets are usually served as a snack, in syrup or a milky sauce.

▲ Raita, a northern Indian dish of yoghurt mixed with cucumber, mint and spices. Raita is served with rice, spicy dishes and salads.

▼ A traditional English cream tea consists of clotted cream served with summer fruit or scones.

The Asian dessert halva is a cake made from semolina and milk, flavoured with raisins, almonds and spices. Shrikhand is another dessert, made from sweetened, flavoured yoghurt. Kulfi is a kind of ice-cream, made with milk, sugar, nuts and spices.

Milk customs

Since ancient times, milk has been a symbol of wealth and fertility. In the Bible, rich countries are described as 'flowing with milk and honey'. History tells us that in ancient Egypt, the wealthy bathed in asses' milk.

In some parts of the world, tribal peoples still measure wealth by the number of cattle they own. The Surma of Ethiopia and the Maasai of Tanzania and Kenya are tribal peoples who feed on the milk and blood of their cattle. Cows are counted as wealth in marriage settlements, and milk is used in ceremonies such as burial, where it is poured into the ears of the dead as a final blessing.

▲ Maasai men in traditional dress. For some tribal peoples like the Maasai, cattle are important possessions.

Cows and milk appear in the religions and legends of the Mediterranean and West Asia. The cows which were painted on cave walls in Palaeolithic (Old Stone Age) times were probably believed to have magical powers to help fertility. In the art of ancient Egypt, cows are symbols of the goddesses Hathor and Isis.

In the Hindu religion, cows are sacred animals which cannot be harmed or killed. In India, sacred cows can be seen wandering in the streets of towns and cities. For peoples who do not eat meat because of their religion, such as Hindus and some Sikhs, milk is especially important because it is a good source of protein.

◀ This cow is decorated for a religious ceremony in Rajastan, India.

▼ A woman in Mongolia milking a horse. The milk will be fermented for drinking.

The ancient tradition of making fermented milk drinks began with nomadic tribes of Europe and Asia. These drinks include Icelandic skyr, Scandinavian taetta, skuta from Chile, tarbo from the Balkans, and kefir and kumiss from Asia and the Middle East.

25

Milk recipes for you to try

Crispy cheese toast

To serve two people you will need:

- 2 tablespoons milk
- 25 g breadcrumbs
- 1 egg
- 1 teaspoon mustard
- a pinch of salt

- a pinch of cayenne pepper
- 75 g cheddar cheese, grated
- 2 slices of toast, buttered
- 1 tablespoon parsley, chopped

1 Gently heat the milk in a saucepan. When the milk is warm, soak the breadcrumbs in it.

2 Beat the egg and mix together with the milk and breadcrumbs. Season with the mustard, salt and cayenne pepper.

3 Stir in the grated cheese.

4 Spread on to the buttered toast. Place the toast on a baking tray and roast in the oven at 200° Centigrade (400° Fahrenheit, gas mark 6) for 20 minutes.

Sprinkle with the parsley and serve.

Apple pancakes

To serve four people you will need:

4 cooking apples, peeled and sliced
$\frac{1}{2}$ teaspoon cinnamon
50 g brown sugar
250 ml milk
1 tablespoon melted butter
1 egg
a pinch of salt
100 g plain flour

1 Put the sliced apples in a saucepan with the cinnamon, sugar and 1–2 tablespoons of water. Cover the pan and cook gently until the apples are soft. Stir from time to time to stop the apples sticking to the pan.

2 While the apples are cooking, make the pancakes. Sift the flour and salt into a mixing bowl. Make a well in the middle of the flour and break the egg into it, adding the melted butter and half the milk.

3 Beat with a spoon until the mixture is smooth and creamy, then gradually beat in the rest of the milk.

4 Grease a frying pan with a little butter. Ask an adult to help you to heat the pan. When it is hot, pour in two or three tablespoons of the batter. Tilt the pan carefully so the batter covers the bottom.

5 Cook the pancake until one side is golden brown, then turn it over carefully using a spatula and cook the other side. Turn the pancake on to a plate. Repeat until you have used up all the batter.

When the pancakes are cooked, spoon some of the apple mix on to each one, and fold it over. Sprinkle with sugar and cinnamon and serve hot with cream, soured cream or crème fraiche.

29

Glossary

aerosol A container that uses gas to spray out its contents as a mist of fine droplets.

airtight Sealed so that air cannot get in or out.

Amerindians American Indians, the original peoples of America.

bacteria Tiny plants that can cause disease but can also be useful.

buttermilk The liquid that is left after churning butter.

carbohydrate Starchy or sugary foods which give energy.

churn To move milk around in a churn or machine until butter forms.

churns Cans used to carry milk, or machines for making butter.

creameries Modern factories for dairy products.

culture Harmless bacteria which grow and ferment milk.

dairy foods Foods that are made from milk.

enzymes Substances which help to break down food into nutrients.

evaporation Heating to drive water off solids.

fermented What happens when a culture is added.

fertility The ability to breed and produce young.

gourds A kind of fruit hollowed out and used as bowls.

junkets Sweetened and flavoured milk curds.

laboratory A place where scientific research takes place.

lactose Milk sugar.

mammals Animals which feed their young on milk.

medieval from the period of the Middle Ages.

Middle Ages The time in history from the fifth to the fifteenth century.

milk floats Vehicles used to deliver milk.

milking parlour Place where cows are milked and the milk is stored ready for collection.

milk solids What is left after milk has evaporated.

minerals Substances found in some foods that we need to keep us healthy.

nervous system A network of special cells in the body.

nomadic Peoples who move from place to place rather than settling in one place.

nutritious Containing goodness.

protein Part of food we need to build and repair our bodies.

rennet Animal or vegetable substance which contains enzymes to curdle milk.

sacred Having religious importance to some people.

saffron The bright yellow part of the crocus flower used for colour and flavour in cooking.

silage Hay or straw that has been stored.

sterilized Treated to kill bacteria.

tanker A vehicle used to transport large amounts of liquid.

tribe A group of people who are related to each other or come from the same culture.

vats Tanks, usually used for holding liquid.

vegetarian Eating no meat.

vitamins Substances found in some foods which we need to keep us healthy.

Books to read

For younger readers:

Spring on the Farm by Jillian Powell (Wayland, 1996)

For older readers:

Farming by Roy Woodcock (Wayland, 1996)

The following may still be available in your local library:

Focus on Dairy Produce by Richard Clark (Wayland, 1985)

Food from Dairy and Farmyard by Jacqueline Dineen (Young Library Ltd, 1985)

Let's Visit a Dairy Farm by Sarah Doughty and Diana Bentley (Wayland, 1989)

Milk by Annabelle Dixon (A & C Black, 1987)

For further information on milk and dairy foods, contact

The National Dairy Council
5–7 John Princes Street
London W1M OAP

Index